GOD IS MY LIFE

GOD IS MY LIFE

The Story of Our Lady of Gethsemani

Photographs by SHIRLEY BURDEN

Introduction by THOMAS MERTON

REYNAL & COMPANY, NEW YORK

INTRODUCTION

PLACES, LIKE PERSONS, have their identity. And especially
a place, like this one, where so many persons have passed through
joy, suffering, confusion and clarity, into the mystery of God.
Places, like persons, lose the sense of their own identity.
They tend to fabricate for themselves a character, and it is with
this unconscious substitute for reality that they go out to meet
other men. Other men obligingly accept the substitute. And even
the camera is often too ready to acquiesce in an illusion. The
camera does not lie—but a lot depends on where you point it.
Not often does the camera know where to look, to find the
real identity of a person, of a place, of a monastery. One may even
ask: Can such things ever be seen, and recorded?
I live in the monastery where these pictures were taken.
What I recognize, when I look at them, is more than the buildings
and fields with which I am familiar. More than what the monks
think of as their monastery.
Do you, perhaps, imagine that the monastic life is romantic?
It is not. It is terribly prosaic. We who live in it are more aware
than others that the ideal and the real are very far apart. We spend
much, often too much time, struggling to reconcile what cannot,
and need not, be reconciled. Perhaps we must confess, that
some of us came here with a kind of secret, romantic enthusiasm
in our hearts: and that we are angry because it is all shot.
And now a man, an artist, comes along with a camera and shows
us, beyond a doubt, that the real monastery, the one that is
so obvious that we no longer see it, the one that has become so
familiar that we have not even looked at it for years, is not
only beautiful, but romantically beautiful. It is romantic even in
the ordinariness, the banality that we ourselves tend to reject.

What a lesson is in this simple fact! Our partial, fabricated
self: the self that wants to be at the same time angelic and up to
date, is pitifully imaginary. The rain-washed angel in the secular
cemetery is there to remind us of our folly.

In a place where things are seldom thrown away, where ladders
remain for weeks in a corner after the work is done; where aged
and sentimental statues do not disappear but move gradually
backward and outward into shops, sheds, attics, barns or
greenhouses; in such a place, one lives amid the accumulated
memories of past mistakes. Those who are not humble hate
their past and push it out of sight, just as they also cut down the
growing and green things that spring up inexhaustibly
even in the present.

But the struggle goes on, silent and inexorable. And when
we think we have won a victory for our partial conception of
newness and of order, we find that the honeysuckle has
triumphed over the abandoned gate; the ivy is coming in the
windows; the hollyhocks are running wild among the clotheslines;
the trumpet vines have crawled up to the very feet of
St. Joseph; the discarded church bell in the vegetable garden
provides a magnificent frame for the distant steeple and
the weeds grow up everywhere full of tiny flowers. Then we
remember that it is the honeysuckle, the hollyhocks and
the rest that are really alive and that they have something very
appropriate to say about the mercy of God. For His Mercy
covers everything and turns mistakes, oversights and
forgetfulness into a riot of new creation.

Now for once, almost for the first time the camera
has caught sight of all this fugitive and symbolic beauty in the
very heart of all that is, to us, most ordinary.

Under the wonderful, moving mountains of cumulus cloud, amid
the tall grasses and the shallow waters of the creeks,
in the hayfields, the barns, the shops, the young monks work
and sweat and laugh and are bewildered. The old monks

plod on in emptiness, saying nothing, now no longer because it
is the rule but because they have lost interest in speech.
The young ones and the old ones go into the church and pray,
perhaps, leaning sadly against a brick wall. Or they go meditate
under a tree. Or they read by a pond. Or they find
for themselves corners and sit in them, face to face with
questions that have no answer.
Meanwhile, the water moves, the leaves move, things grow in
silence, life reaches out all around us. The silence of God embraces
us, consoles us, answers our questions (once we have the sense to
stop asking). And the flowers bloom everywhere, the high weeds
wave in the sun, the birds chant in the swinging green
heavens which are the trees; and all this has much to say to
anyone able to listen. It is all liturgy because it is all mercy.
Then, at the height of the summer, with the sun boiling the
creeks and baking the cow-trampled mud as hard as rock, the
liturgical life of the monastery bursts into its own most luxuriant
flower. It is the Feast of Corpus Christi. The feast of that
inexpressible Sacrament of Divine Mercy in which Christ dwells
in our midst in lowliness and splendor. The feast of that
Sacrament which is made of the wheat of our fields, changed into
the Body of the Son of God. To honor Him, the fields are
ransacked of flowers, the gardens are stripped. Even the weeds
come into their own: they have their place in the flower mosaics
on the cloister floor where the hidden Christ will pass by,
secret in His obviousness, King and Host.
Such things, and many more, even deeper mysteries, this camera
has seen. And yet not everything is in these pages. For this book is
not intended as documentation. It is a work of art, and in a work
of art what is not said is just as important, if not more so, than
what is explicit. Perhaps if more things were shown here,
less would be evident. What we have, at any rate, is a Trappist
monastery, the oldest and largest one in the western world seen not
as a sociological phenomenon but as a religious mystery.

—THOMAS MERTON

It was through Him
    that all things
came into being
    and without Him came nothing
that has come to be

There are many kinds of love
and many degrees of love.
This is about a love
I found at Our Lady of Gethsemani--

In 1805 thirty-seven Trappist Monks came from France to build a Monastery in the United States

They wandered far
and suffered much
for Our Lady of Gethsemani

Some gave all they had

When first I went there
     I wondered
how man could give his life to God

As I drew near
I heard the voices of men singing

The incense of flowers
filled the heavens
 with their praise

On a hilltop
a man called Joseph
   stood alone
      with the Child in his arms

What I saw.
was of God

What I felt
    let His words be heard

How narrow the gate
and close the way
that leads to life
and few there are
who find it

Blessed are your eyes, for they see
and your ears for they hear
    for Amen, I say to you
many prophets and just men
have longed to see what you see
and they have not seen it;
    and to hear
and they have not heard it

And everyone who has left house or brothers
 or sisters
 or father or mother
 or wife or children
 or lands
 for My sake
shall receive a hundred-fold
and shall possess
 life everlasting

Do not lay up for yourselves treasures on earth
    where rust and moth consume
    and where thieves break in and steal
but lay up for yourselves treasures in Heaven
    where neither rust nor moth consumes
    nor thieves break in and steal
for where thy treasure is
    there also will thy heart be

In my world
   I count the days and nights

Here
    time has no meaning
their goal is eternity

Let us lay aside the works of darkness
and put on the armor of light

And we saw His glory:
  Glory as of the Only Begotten of the Father
    full of grace
    and of the truth

He is not the God of the dead
    but of the living

Only the spirit gives life
 the flesh is of no avail.
The words I have been speaking to you
 are spirit and life

Lift up your eyes and behold
    that the fields are already white for the harvest
and he who reaps
    receives a wage
    and gathers fruit unto life everlasting
so that the sower and the reaper
    may rejoice together

He fed them with Bread from Heaven

Like men I know.
  they live and work

Yet not like other men

Their thoughts are of God

Their joy
    the Feast of Corpus Christi

from the forest
   they gather a cover of green;

from the flowers
a rainbow.

Make ready the way of the Lord.
Make straight His paths.
Every valley shall be filled
  and every mountain and hill
  shall be brought low;
  and the crooked ways shall be made straight
  and the rough ways smooth;

and all mankind
shall see the salvation of God

He who comes to Me
will never be hungry

He who has faith in Me
    will never know thirst

He who loses his life for My sake
will find it

I am with you all days
even unto the consummation of the world

Heaven and earth will pass away
but My words will not pass away

Come follow. Me

I am the Way
   and the Truth
      and the Life

POSTSCRIPT

A LOT MORE COULD BE SAID about The Abbey of
Our Lady of Gethsemani than has been said in this book. More
pictures could have been taken, and were, but they did not
convey what I eventually felt about Gethsemani.
I find it difficult to work to a script, or even an outline.
After a theme has been chosen, pictures, to me, should suggest the
direction of the story. This was especially true of "God is my Life."
When Captain Edward Steichen, curator of photography for
the Museum of Modern Art in New York, first asked me if I wanted
to photograph the life at the Abbey, I was not too sure.
Finally, the thought of fourteen hundred acres, two hundred men,
and God, proved too much for my curiosity and I accepted.
From the beginning, I had a pre-conceived idea of what Gethsemani
would be like, I had seen many pictures of beautiful old
monasteries in Europe, and I was sure it would look much the same.
This was not the case. From the outside, Gethsemani is
neither ugly, nor is it beautiful. The buildings you see, and the many
daily jobs you watch the monks perform, have little to do
with its meaning. What transforms it is an overpowering desire
on the part of these men to be with God now, and for all eternity.
You cannot see it, but you can feel it, and it surrounds you
in a wonderful way. I believe I was aware of this some time before
I really understood it. One night I woke about 2 A.M.
From somewhere far away, I could hear the sound of chanting
voices. As I lay in the darkness, listening, the real meaning
of Gethsemani came over me.

I thought of the river I had wanted to photograph the day before,
but had not, because it was like many another river in the world.
I realized it was beautiful, not because it was at Gethsemani, and
not because it was a river. It was beautiful, because it reminded
me of God, and that was the essence of Gethsemani.
From then on, I felt surer of what I was doing. I knew a story
would eventually evolve if the pictures I took reflected the soul
rather than the body.
When I finished I was sad. I must leave men I could not soon forget,
and a way of life few understand, and fewer would have the
conviction and courage to live.

SHIRLEY BURDEN

DATE

Due	Due	Due

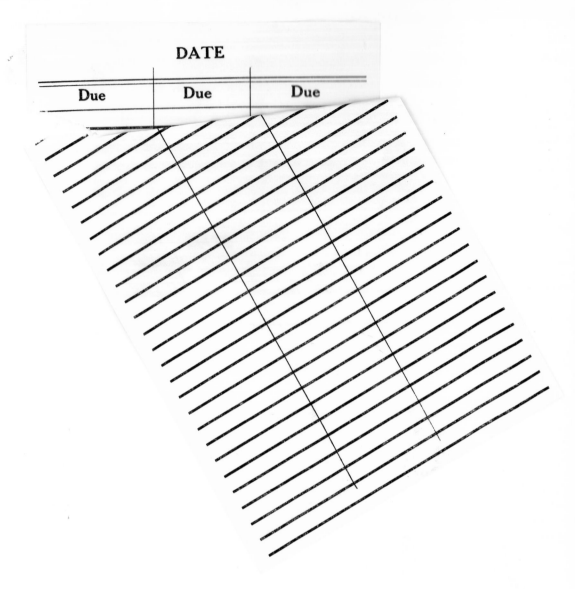